Quick Start Guides

The Es

SUGAR FREE
FAMILY
COOKBOOK

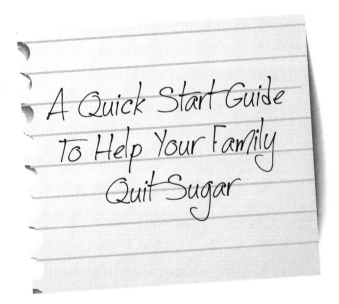

A Quick Start Guide To Help Your Family Quit Sugar

Over 100 Healthy And Delicious Family Friendly Recipes

First published in 2015 by Erin Rose Publishing

Text and illustration copyright © 2015 Erin Rose Publishing

Design: Julie Anson

ISBN: 978-0-9933204-3-9

A CIP record for this book is available from the British Library.

DISCLAIMER: This book is for informational purposes only and not intended as a substitute for the medical advice, diagnosis or treatment of a physician or qualified healthcare provider. The reader should consult a physician before undertaking a new health care regime and in all matters relating to his/her health, and particularly with respect to any symptoms that may require diagnosis or medical attention.

While every care has been taken in compiling the recipes for this book we cannot accept responsibility for any problems which arise as a result of preparing one of the recipes. The author and publisher disclaim responsibility for any adverse effects that may arise from the use or application of the recipes in this book. Some of the recipes in this book include nuts and eggs. If you have an egg or nut allergy it's important to avoid these.

CONTENTS

Recipes
Breakfast

Lunch

Dinner

Desserts, Sweet Treats & Snacks 89

INTRODUCTION

If you want to give your family healthy sugar-free meals which are exciting and packed with flavour but don't know what to cook to keep everyone happy, then this **Quick Start Guide To Sugar-Free Family Cooking** is a great place to begin!

Inside this book you'll find fabulous, creative recipes which you and your family can devour guilt-free, with plenty of sweet tasting dishes and desserts you can all enjoy! Because we've all had the craving for something sweet, even after a delicious, filling meal, we know that's when sugar-cravings can break the healthiest of diets, even when we aren't hungry!

Most people now know the biggest threat to our nation's health is sugar and that it's been linked with a myriad of chronic illnesses, not just limited to obesity and diabetes. It's been depleting our energy and affecting our mood in ways we hadn't realised.

So why is this such a major issue now? Because, sugar in various forms, has been added in huge quantities to many of our everyday foods, not just to cakes, chocolate bars and cookies. Even savoury foods are laced with sugar which may not have been obvious from the ingredients list. We've been drip fed a highly addictive substance to keep us coming back for more. Eating sugar creates an insatiable desire for more sweet things. It's a perpetual cycle of cravings and blood sugar imbalances. The initial rush of energy from sugar creates a lull and the need for another fix.

In this book we'll help you identify hidden sugars in foods which are marketed as being 'healthy' or 'low fat' which often have hideous amounts of sugar added to compensate for the removal of other ingredients such as fat, which is not as harmful for us as we thought. So, going sugar-free isn't just about cutting out the obvious sweet treats but becoming knowledgeable about where the devious sugars are lurking.

The average daily sugar intake per person is 93.2g in the U.K. and 125.4g in the U.S. The recommended daily sugar intake is no more than 36g a day, which is still 9 teaspoons! If you're thinking this doesn't apply to you because you don't take sugar in your coffee or add it to your breakfast cereal, note that most sugar is consumed unknowingly. It might be worth keeping a diary for one week, recording everything you eat and its sugar content. You will be surprised!

Now we're taking back control of what we eat and looking for the key to break free from the sugar-trap. It can be daunting, especially if you have a family who want their sweet treats but you know they are consuming too much sugar. You know the path to good health is not sugar coated and you know that by going sugar-free you're doing a great thing and investing in you and your family's future health and well-being. We want to make it easy for you and your family. If you're ready to make the change, let's get started!

Getting Started

The first thing you need to know is what foods to avoid. You'll need to be your own detective and weed out the problem foods so familiarise yourself with what you need to avoid. Yes, with some foods it will be obvious that they contain sugar but others less so.

When you begin going sugar-free, the less sugar you have the sooner the cravings will subside. Don't fool yourself into believing you won't crave sugary foods but remember that it will pass in a few days. Cheating will prolong cravings and make it more difficult for you to stay sugar-free.

Don't make the mistake of eating large quantities of fruit – it's a form of sugar. Likewise for dried fruits, which people often earmark for a handy snack, but dried fruit has a higher concentration of sugar.

Eat fat. Yes, you did just read that! Fat is not only satisfying but it has nutritional benefits which sugar doesn't. So cubes of cheese, an avocado or a slice of bacon can keep hunger away until your next meal.

What NOT To Eat:

Any food containing sugar – read all the labels.

- Avoid all fizzy and sugary drinks, including diet drinks with artificial sweeteners such as, aspartame, xylitol, sucralose, cyclamates, saccharin, acesulfame potassium.
- Avoid dried fruit, including apricots, dates, raisins, sultanas, apples, bananas, mango, pineapple and figs.
- Pure or concentrated fruit juices.
- Cakes, biscuits, muesli, granola, muffins, cereal bars and sweets.
- Breakfast cereals (where sugar is added to the ingredients).
- Sucrose
- Maltose
- Dextrose
- Corn syrup
- Glucose syrup
- Fructose
- High fructose corn syrup
- Agave syrup or nectar
- Honey
- Jam
- Golden syrup
- Maple syrup
- Treacle
- Molasses
- Ready-made sauces like relish, ketchup and barbecue sauce.

How To Read The Labels

Check all your food labels. Even buying cooked chicken portions at the super-market can up your sugar intake. Those baked beans which the kids love may have large quantities of sugar added to the sauce. Be very careful of sauces and dressing as often sugar is the first ingredients listed, which means it is the highest quantity!

Sugar can also be listed under the names below. Avoid these.

- Invert sugar syrup
- Cane juice crystals
- Dextrin
- Dextrose
- Glucose syrup
- Sucrose
- Fructose syrup
- Maltodextrin
- Barley malt
- Beet sugar
- High fructose corn syrup
- Corn syrup
- Date sugar
- Palm sugar or coconut sugar
- Malt syrup
- Dehydrated fruit juice

- Fruit juice concentrate
- Carob syrup
- Golden syrup
- Refiners syrup
- Ethyl maltol
- Jaggery

The Fructose Facts

It's a common misconception that the more fruit you eat the better it is for your health, but that's not strictly true. Fruit contains fructose (fruit sugar) which is basically stored in the liver and not utilised by the body straight away. Keep your fruit intake to no more than 2 pieces per day. Although there is a difference between fructose which occurs naturally and that which has undergone an industrial process that makes it harmful to the body, it's worth noting that fruit should be eaten WITH its fibre, which not only increases it's nutritional benefit but it slows the sugar absorption rate. High fructose corn syrup is a factory produced substance which is linked with various health problems and should be avoided.

Sweeteners

One of the biggest shocks most recently has been that agave syrup, marketed as being low GI (which it is) and healthy is as harmful as high fructose corn syrup because it has an exceptionally high fructose content. In this book we have avoided the use of agave and other types of artificial sweeteners which have been linked to health problems. For many people, honey is still a favourite because it's natural and manuka honey particularly has anti-viral properties. But please be aware that honey is a form of sugar and it contains fructose and glucose; but for many people it's a preferable alternative. The main difference between fructose and glucose is that the body utilises glucose immediately whereas fructose is stored and becomes fat.

We don't use potentially harmful artificial sweeteners in our recipes and there is no added sugar; we really believe that a healthy diet is based on clean eating, avoiding processed foods and keeping sugar consumption to a minimum. We do give you the option to use stevia, a sweetener extracted from the Stevia Rebaudiana plant which has no known harmful effects.

Recipes

Sugar-free Family Cooking

Our sugar-free recipes are designed for families and most of the portion sizes are based on a family of four. There are some exceptions to this, particularly in the breakfast section where the smoothies are based on servings for two people. This is because breakfast can be notoriously difficult time to provide what each person wants and many of us don't eat breakfast together. Importantly, don't skip breakfast as it's really important to balance blood sugar levels and provide energy to kick-start your day.

Get creative and make it easier for yourself, put the right kind of temptation in your way: include in your diet something which you can really look forward to. Coconut is an amazing treat - it's a sweet, satisfying, ingredient that won't play havoc with blood sugar levels.

When you cook using fresh wholesome ingredients, you won't feel the need to add unnecessary sugar which is added to the sauces of many convenience meals. While you are going sugar-free your taste buds will adapt to subtler flavours and you may be surprised to find some foods seem too sweet. However, it may take a little time and the longer sugar is avoided the greater your overall success in kicking the white stuff for good.

A little trick you can use is to add a pinch of salt to a dish, savoury or sweet, to fool your taste buds into thinking something is sweeter than it actually is. It's worth making a batch of something from the sweet treats section and storing it.

BREAKFAST

Egg & Bacon Pie

Ingredients

100g (3 ½ oz) Cheddar cheese, grated (shredded)
8 eggs
4 slices streaky bacon, roughly chopped
4 spring onions (scallions), finely chopped
2 tomatoes, thickly sliced
150mls (5fl oz) double cream (heavy cream)

SERVES 4-6

Method

Whisk together the cream and eggs in a bowl. Add in the cheese, bacon and spring onions (scallions). Grease and line a baking tin or dish with greaseproof paper. Pour in the egg mixture and stir it to disperse the cheese. Add the slices of tomato to the top. Transfer to an oven, preheated to 180C/360F and cook for 40 minutes, or until the eggs are set and thoroughly cooked. Can be served hot or cold.

Cheese & Courgette (Zucchini) Mini Omelettes

Ingredients

50g (2oz) Cheddar cheese, grated (shredded)
4 large eggs
1 small courgette (zucchini), finely chopped
Freshly ground black pepper

SERVES 4

Method

Whisk the eggs then add the grated cheese and black pepper. Add the courgette (zucchini) and mix well. Lightly grease a muffin tin. Pour in the egg mixture. Bake in the oven at 180C/360F for around 20 minutes until the eggs are set. You can also try other fillings such as spinach, tomatoes, ham, chicken, prawns, mushrooms, spring onions (scallions), olives, peas and feta cheese.

Vegetable & Egg Rosti

Ingredients

450g (1lb) potatoes, peeled

4 eggs

2 carrots, grated (shredded)

2 tablespoons fresh parsley, chopped

1 leek, finely chopped

2 tablespoons olive oil

SERVES 4

Method

Grate (shred) the potatoes then squeeze out the liquid and pat them dry with a paper towel. Heat the olive oil in a frying pan, add the leek and cook for 1 minute. Add the grated (shredded) carrots and potatoes, spreading them out in the pan. Cook for 10-12 minutes until crisp and golden. In the meantime, preheat the grill. Transfer the frying pan to under the grill and cook until the top is golden. Use the back of a spoon and make 4 egg-size indentations in the rosti. Crack an egg into each indentation. Sprinkle with parsley and return the frying pan to the heat. Cook for 4-5 minutes until the eggs are set.

Baked Egg Avocados

Ingredients

4 eggs
2 large avocados, halved and stones removed
1 tablespoon fresh parsley, finely chopped
Sea salt
Freshly ground black pepper

SERVES
2-4

Method

Place half of an avocado in a ramekin dish with the hollow facing upwards. Crack an egg into the each avocado. You may need to remove a little avocado flesh to get the whole egg in if it is particularly large. Sprinkle with parsley, salt and pepper. Bake in an oven, preheated to 220C/440F and cook for 20 minutes until the eggs have set. Serve immediately.

Mexican Bean & Mushroom Omelette

Ingredients

200g (7oz) tinned mixed beans, drained
200g (7oz) mushrooms, chopped
8 eggs, beaten
1 green pepper (bell pepper), chopped
1 red pepper (bell pepper), chopped
2 tablespoons olive oil
Sprinkling of chilli powder

SERVES 4-6

Method

Heat the olive oil in a pan and add the mushrooms, peppers (bell peppers) and beans. Cook for 3-4 minutes until the mushrooms and peppers have softened. Remove them and set them aside. Pour the beaten eggs into the pan. Once they begin to set, return the mushrooms, peppers and beans and spread them onto the eggs. Sprinkle with chilli powder and serve.

Pear Porridge

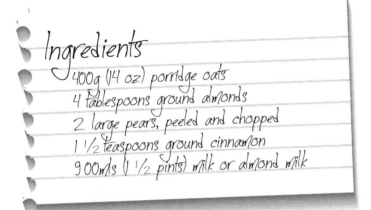

Ingredients

- 400g (14 oz) porridge oats
- 4 tablespoons ground almonds
- 2 large pears, peeled and chopped
- 1 1/2 teaspoons ground cinnamon
- 900mls (1 1/2 pints) milk or almond milk

SERVES 4

Method

In a saucepan, cook all of the ingredients, apart from ground almonds, for 5 minutes or until it thickens. Serve topped with a sprinkling of ground almonds.

Berry & Coconut Porridge

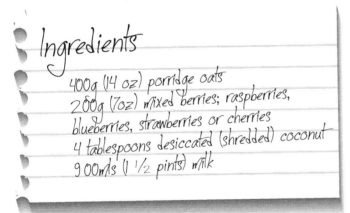

Ingredients

- 400g (14 oz) porridge oats
- 200g (7oz) mixed berries; raspberries, blueberries, strawberries or cherries
- 4 tablespoons desiccated (shredded) coconut
- 900mls (1 1/2 pints) milk

SERVES 4

Method

Place the oats, coconut and milk into a saucepan and cook until the mixture thickens. Serve the porridge into a bowl and top it off with the berries..

Mozzarella & Basil Frittata

Ingredients

125g (4oz) mozzarella cheese, grated (shredded)
6 large eggs
1 large handful of basil, chopped
2 tablespoons olive oil
Sea salt
Freshly ground black pepper

SERVES 4

Method

Crack the eggs into a bowl and whisk them. Stir in the fresh basil and season with salt and pepper. Heat the olive oil in a frying pan and pour in the egg mixture. Cook them for 5-6 minutes or until they are set. Sprinkle on the grated mozzarella and place the pan under a hot grill (broiler) until the top is golden.

Chicken & Green Pepper Breakfast Pots

Ingredients

100g (3 ½ oz) cooked chicken, finely chopped (leftovers is fine)
4 large eggs
4 teaspoons crème fraiche
1 green pepper (bell pepper), finely chopped
1 tablespoon fresh chives, finely chopped

SERVES 4

Method

Lightly grease 4 ramekin dishes then line them with pieces of chicken and green pepper (bell pepper). Crack an egg into each ramekin dish. Add a teaspoon of crème fraiche and a sprinkling of chopped chives. Place them in the oven at 180C/360F for 16 minutes for soft yolks and longer if you like your eggs completely set.

Mint & Strawberry Smoothie

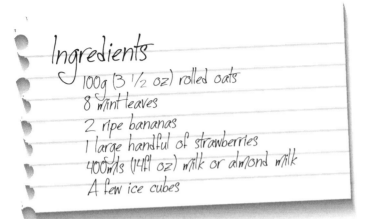

Ingredients

- 100g (3 ½ oz) rolled oats
- 8 mint leaves
- 2 ripe bananas
- 1 large handful of strawberries
- 400mls (14fl oz) milk or almond milk
- A few ice cubes

SERVES
2

Method

Place all the ingredients into a blender and blitz. If your blender doesn't process ice you can always crush the ice and add it after blending.

Orange & Ginger Smoothie

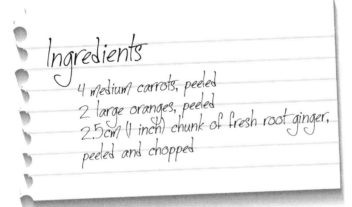

Ingredients

- 4 medium carrots, peeled
- 2 large oranges, peeled
- 2.5cm (1 inch) chunk of fresh root ginger, peeled and chopped

SERVES
2

Method

Place the ingredients into a blender with enough water to cover the ingredients (or juicer if you prefer) and process until smooth.

Mango Smoothie

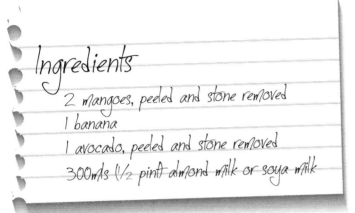

Ingredients

- 2 mangoes, peeled and stone removed
- 1 banana
- 1 avocado, peeled and stone removed
- 300mls (½ pint) almond milk or soya milk

SERVES
2

Method

Place the ingredients into a blender and blitz until smooth.

Blueberry & Spinach Smoothie

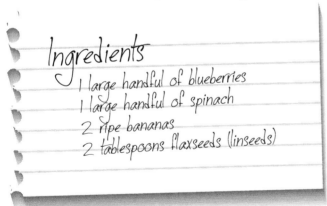

Ingredients

- 1 large handful of blueberries
- 1 large handful of spinach
- 2 ripe bananas
- 2 tablespoons flaxseeds (linseeds)

SERVES
2

Method

Place all the ingredients into a blender with enough water to cover them and blitz until smooth.

LUNCH

Minestrone Soup

Ingredients

450g (1lb) butterbeans, drained and rinsed
250g (9 oz) passata
25g (1oz) Parmesan cheese, grated (shredded)
4 tomatoes, chopped
2 carrots, finely chopped
2 onions, finely chopped
2 cloves of garlic, crushed
1 large courgette (zucchini) finely chopped
1 tablespoon fresh basil leaves, chopped
750mls (1 1/4 pints) vegetable stock (broth)
1 tablespoon olive oil
Sea salt
Freshly ground black pepper

SERVES 4

Method

Place the tomatoes in hot water for a minute or so then remove the skin and seeds and chop it finely. Heat the olive oil in a pan and add the carrots, onions, courgette (zucchini) and garlic. Cook for 3 minutes. Pour in the passata and stock (broth). Bring to the boil, reduce the heat and simmer for 10 minutes. Add in the butterbeans, tomatoes and chopped basil and warm them through. Season with salt and pepper. Serve into bowls and sprinkle with Parmesan.

Sweet Potato & Lentil Soup

Ingredients

- 450g (1lb) sweet potatoes, peeled and diced
- 200g (7oz) red lentils
- 4 large tomatoes, skinned, de-seeded & chopped
- 1 carrot, chopped
- 1 large onion, chopped
- 1 red pepper (bell pepper), chopped
- 1 clove garlic, chopped
- 1 tablespoon olive oil
- 2 tablespoons fresh basil, chopped
- 1 litre (1 3/4 pints) stock (broth)

SERVES 4

Method

Heat the olive oil in a saucepan, add the onion and garlic and cook for 4 minutes. Add in the sweet potatoes, carrots, lentils, tomatoes and red pepper (bell pepper) then pour in the stock (broth). Bring to the boil, reduce the heat and simmer for 30 minutes or until the vegetables are soft. Allow to cool for 10 minutes then using a hand blender or food processor blend slightly but leave the soup chunky. Add in the fresh basil leaves and heat further if required before serving.

Pear & Celeriac Soup

Ingredients

2 pears, cored, peeled and chopped
1 celeriac, peeled and chopped
1 onion, chopped
2.5cm (1 inch) chunk fresh root ginger
600mls (1 pint) vegetable stock (broth)
2 tablespoons olive oil
Freshly ground black pepper

SERVES 4-6

Method

Heat the olive oil in a saucepan, add the onion, celeriac, pears, ginger and cook for 5 minutes. Pour in the vegetable stock (broth) bring to the boil, reduce the heat and simmer for 20-25 minutes. Using a hand blender or food processor, blend the soup until it's smooth. You can add extra stock (broth) or hot water to make the soup thinner if you wish. Season with pepper then serve into bowls.

Chicken & Lentil Soup

Ingredients

400g (14oz) cooked chicken, leftovers are great
75g (3oz) cauliflower florets
200g (7oz) mushrooms, chopped
200g (7oz) red lentils
1 carrot, chopped
1 onion, chopped
1 courgette (zucchini) chopped
1 red pepper (bell pepper), chopped
1 clove of garlic
1200mls (2 pints) chicken stock (broth)
1 tablespoon olive oil

**SERVES
4**

Method

Heat the olive oil in a saucepan, add the onion and garlic and cook for 4 minutes. Stir in the red pepper (bell pepper), cauliflower, carrot, lentils and mushrooms. Pour in the stock (broth). Bring to the boil, reduce the heat and simmer for 20 minutes. Add in the courgette (zucchini) and chicken. Cook for another 5-10 minutes. Serve and enjoy.

Turkey & Blue Cheese Soup

SERVES 4

Ingredients

350g (12oz) cooked turkey meat (leftovers are fine)

150g (5oz) blue cheese

4 tablespoons butter

1 onion, chopped

1 leek, chopped

1 tablespoon fresh tarragon leaves, chopped

600mls (1 pint) chicken stock (broth)

150mls (5fl oz) double cream (heavy cream)

Method

Heat the butter in a saucepan, add the onion and leek and cook until softened. Add the turkey and stock (broth) to the pan and bring it to the boil. Reduce the heat and simmer for 10 minutes, stirring occasionally. Allow the soup to cool slightly then using a hand blender or food processor blend the soup until it is chunky and smooth. Stir in the blue cheese, double cream (heavy cream) and the chopped tarragon. Heat and stir the soup until warmed through. Serve and enjoy.

Winter Spiced Pumpkin Soup

Ingredients

- 1 kg (2 ¼ lb) pumpkin
- 25g (1oz) butter
- 1 onion, chopped
- ¼ teaspoon nutmeg
- ½ teaspoon cinnamon
- 600ml (1 pint) vegetable stock (broth)
- Sea salt
- Freshly ground black pepper

SERVES 6-8

Method

Cut open the pumpkin, remove the seeds and discard. Cut the flesh into cubes. Heat the butter in a pan and add the onion. Cook until it becomes soft. Add to the pan the pumpkin and the stock (broth). Bring to the boil, reduce the heat and simmer for 30 minutes. Transfer to a food processor or use a hand blender to make a puree from the soup. Return to the pan and add the nutmeg, cinnamon, salt and pepper.

Prawn & Coconut Soup

Ingredients

450g (1lb) prawns (shrimp), peeled and de-veined
4 cloves garlic, crushed
4cm (2 inch) chunk of fresh ginger
4 teaspoons lemongrass paste/2 inner stalks, finely chopped
1 teaspoon curry powder
1 lime, quartered for garnish
1 tablespoon fresh coriander (cilantro)
1/2 teaspoon chilli flakes
400mls (14fl oz) vegetable stock (broth)
750mls (1 1/4 pints) coconut milk
2 tablespoons olive oil
Sea salt, freshly ground black pepper

SERVES 4-6

Method

Heat the olive oil in a large saucepan and add the ginger, garlic, lemongrass, curry powder and chilli flakes. Cook for around 1 minute. Pour in the stock (broth) and mix well. Bring it to the boil, reduce the heat and simmer gently. Add the prawns and cook for 3 minutes. Pour in the coconut milk and warm it through. Season with salt and pepper. Serve in bowls with a wedge of lime and sprinkle with coriander (cilantro).

Crab & Sweetcorn Soup

Ingredients

450g (1lb) sweetcorn
225g (8oz) crabmeat
4 spring onions (scallions) chopped
2 teaspoons cornflour
2 tablespoons fresh coriander (cilantro) chopped
1cm (½ inch) chunk fresh ginger, chopped
1 egg white
1200mls (2 pints) chicken stock (broth)
3 tablespoons soy sauce

SERVES 4

Method

Place the stock (broth), crab meat and sweetcorn into a wok or saucepan, bring to the boil and simmer for 15 minutes. Stir in the ginger, spring onions (scallions) and soy sauce. Simmer for 5 minutes. In a small bowl or cup, mix the cornflour with a tablespoon or two of cold water. Pour the mixture into the soup and stir until the soup thickens slightly. In a bowl, whisk the egg white then pour it into the soup while constantly stirring. Sprinkle in the coriander (cilantro). Serve into bowls.

Fresh Tomato & Basil Soup

SERVES 4

Ingredients

8 large tomatoes, peeled and chopped

1 onion, finely chopped

4 tablespoons fresh basil, chopped

3 tablespoons olive oil

900mls (1 1/2) pints vegetable stock (broth)

Freshly ground black pepper

Method

Heat the oil in a saucepan and add the onion. Cook for 5 minutes until it softens. Add in the tomatoes and simmer gently until the tomatoes are soft and pulpy. Add the stock (broth) and cook for 5 minutes. Season with pepper and add 3 tablespoons of fresh basil. Blend in a food processor or use a hand blender and process until smooth. Stir in the remaining basil and serve.

Chicken, Mushroom & Barley Soup

Ingredients

450g (1lb) chicken breasts, chopped
250g (9 oz) mushrooms, chopped
75g (3oz) pearl barley
2 carrots, chopped
1 onion, chopped
1 leek, chopped
1 tablespoon fresh parsley, chopped
1 tablespoon fresh thyme, chopped
1 tablespoon butter
1 litre (1 3/4 pints) chicken stock (broth)

SERVES 4

Method

Place the barley in a saucepan, cover with boiling water and simmer for 5 minutes. Drain it and set it aside. Heat the butter in a saucepan, add the onion and leek and cook for 4 minutes. Add in the stock (broth) and barley. Bring to the boil, reduce the heat and simmer for 40 minutes. Add the chicken, carrots, mushrooms, parsley and thyme. Cook for around 15-20 minutes until the vegetables have softened.

Avocado & Orange Salad

Ingredients

- 2 large avocados, peeled and stone removed
- 3 oranges, peeled
- 2 teaspoons cardamom pods
- Large handful of watercress
- 2 tablespoons olive oil
- ½ teaspoon ground allspice
- Juice of ½ lime

SERVES 4

Method

Cut the orange flesh from the outer skin to remove the individual segments and place them in a bowl. Slice the avocados and add them to the orange segments. Using the back of a spoon or a mortar and pestle, break the cardamom pods open and remove the tiny seeds. In a bowl, mix together the cardamom seeds with the lime juice, olive oil and allspice. Toss the oranges, avocados and watercress in the dressing then serve.

Garlic Dough Balls

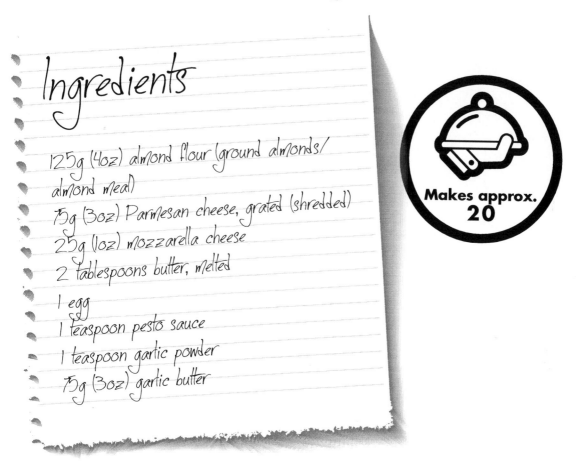

Ingredients

125g (4oz) almond flour (ground almonds/almond meal)

75g (3oz) Parmesan cheese, grated (shredded)

25g (1oz) mozzarella cheese

2 tablespoons butter, melted

1 egg

1 teaspoon pesto sauce

1 teaspoon garlic powder

75g (3oz) garlic butter

Makes approx. 20

Method

Place all of the ingredients, apart from the garlic butter, into a bowl and combine them. Grease and line a baking tray. Scoop out a tablespoon of the mixture and roll it into a ball. Repeat it for the remaining mixture. Transfer it to the oven and bake at 180C/360F for around 20 minutes, or until golden. Spread some garlic butter onto each dough ball. Enjoy warm.

Aubergine (Eggplant) Gratin

SERVES 4-6

Ingredients

50g (2oz) Cheddar cheese, grated (shredded)

4 large ripe tomatoes

2 ripe aubergines (eggplants)

2-3 tablespoons olive oil

Method

Cut the tomatoes into slices and set aside. Thinly slice the aubergines (eggplants) and place them under a hot grill (broiler). Brush with olive oil and cook for 15 minutes turning once. Place the tomato slices and aubergine slices in an oven-proof dish, alternating between slices of each. Cover with the grated cheese. Transfer to the oven and bake at 200C/400F for 15 minutes, or until the cheese is golden. Serve and eat immediately.

Mozzarella Breadsticks

Ingredients

- 300g (11oz) mozzarella cheese, grated (shredded)
- 4 eggs
- 3 cloves of garlic, crushed
- 2 teaspoons dried oregano
- 1 head of cauliflower, grated (shredded)
- Sea salt
- Freshly ground black pepper

SERVES
8

Method

Steam the grated cauliflower until tender and allow it to cool. Place the cauliflower in a bowl and combine it with the eggs, two thirds of the cheese and garlic. Season with salt and pepper. Grease 2 baking sheets. Divide the mixture in half and place it on the baking sheet and press it into a flat rectangular shape. Transfer the baking sheets to the oven and bake at 220C/440F for 20-25 minutes or until slightly golden. Remove them from the oven and sprinkle them with the remaining mozzarella cheese. Return them to the oven for 5 minutes or until the cheese has melted. Cut the breads into sticks or slices and serve.

Quick Chicken Casserole

Ingredients

- 4 chopped chicken breasts
- 3 carrots, chopped
- 2 parsnips, chopped
- ½ turnip, peeled and chopped
- 600mls (1 pint) gravy, ready-mixed or home-made
- 3 tablespoons olive oil
- Freshly ground black pepper

SERVES
4

Method

Heat the oil in a large saucepan. Add the chicken and cook for 5 minutes. Add in the carrots, parsnip and turnip. Cook for around 15 minutes then add in the gravy and cook for 10 minutes. Season with pepper before serving.

Halloumi & Asparagus Salad

SERVES 4

Ingredients

- 250g (9 oz) halloumi cheese, cut into slices
- 2 large bunches asparagus
- 2 large handfuls of spinach leaves
- 1 tablespoon olive oil
- Sea salt
- Freshly ground black pepper

Method

Heat the olive oil in a frying pan, add the asparagus and cook it for 4 minutes or until tender. Remove it and keep it warm. Place the halloumi in the frying pan and cook for 2 minutes on each side until golden. Serve the spinach leaves onto plates and add the asparagus and halloumi slices. Season with salt and pepper.

Baked Cod With Tomatoes & Olives

SERVES 4

Ingredients

650g (1lb 7oz) new potatoes, roughly sliced
450g (1lb) cherry tomatoes
100g (3½ oz) pitted black olives
4 cod fillets
1 onion, roughly chopped
Small handful of fresh basil leaves
150mls (5fl oz) vegetable stock (broth)
3 tablespoons olive oil
Juice of 1 lemon

Method

Place the sliced potatoes and onion into an oven-proof dish. Pour in the vegetable stock (broth) and bake in the oven at 180C/360F for 15 minutes. Remove from the oven and add into cod, tomatoes, olives, lemon juice and olive oil. Return it to the oven and cook for around 15 minutes or until the cod is cooked through. Add extra olive oil or water if necessary. Sprinkle with basil and serve.

Salmon Kebabs

Ingredients

12 cherry tomatoes
9 pitted black olives
4 salmon fillets
4 tablespoons fresh parsley
1 tablespoon olive oil
Rind and juice of a lemon

SERVES 4

Method

Cut the salmon into 4cm (1½ inch) chunks. Place them in a bowl along with just half of the parsley, lemon rind and juice. Cover and allow to marinate for at least 30 minutes. Thread the salmon chunks onto skewers and alternate them with tomatoes and olives. Place the kebabs under a hot grill (broiler) for 10-12 minutes or until the salmon is thoroughly cooked. In a separate bowl mix together the remaining lemon juice, rind and parsley with a tablespoon of olive oil. Serve the kebabs and spoon over the lemon/oil dressing. Serve with rice and green salad.

Lamb Casserole

Ingredients

450g (1lb) lamb steaks, cubed
4 strips of smoky bacon, chopped
4 tablespoons fresh parsley, chopped
3 carrots, roughly chopped
2 onions, roughly chopped
2 garlic cloves, chopped
1 tablespoon plain flour (all-purpose) flour
1 tablespoon tomato purée (paste)
2 tablespoons olive oil
600mls (1 pint lamb, chicken or beef stock (broth)

SERVES 4

Method

Coat the lamb in the flour. Heat the oil in a frying pan, add the lamb and bacon and brown it for 10 minutes. Add in the garlic, carrots and onions and cook for 5 minutes. Pour in the stock (broth) and cook for 20 minutes. Stir in the tomato purée (paste) and parsley. Season if required. Serve with brown rice, quinoa or couscous.

Fried Avocado Wedges & Lime Yogurt Dip

SERVES
2-4

Ingredients

2 large avocados, skin and stone removed and cut
into wedges
200g (7oz) ground almonds (almond flour/almond
meal)
1 egg, beaten
1 tablespoon olive oil

FOR THE DIP:
100g (3½ oz) Greek yogurt
1 tablespoon fresh coriander (cilantro), chopped
Juice of ½ lime

Method

Place the beaten egg in a bowl and place the ground almonds (almond meal/almond
flour) in another bowl. Grease a baking sheet with olive oil. Dip the avocado wedges
in the egg then dredge them in the ground almonds. Lay the wedges out on the baking sheet. Transfer them to the oven and bake at 220C/440F for 10-12 minutes until
golden. Combine the ingredients for the dip in a bowl and mix well. Serve the avocado
wedges hot alongside the dip.

Falafels

Ingredients

- 400g (14oz) tin of chickpeas (garbanzo beans)
- 75g (3oz) mushrooms, chopped
- 50g (2oz) breadcrumbs
- 2 cloves garlic, chopped
- 2 spring onions (scallions) chopped
- 1 egg
- 1 small handful of parsley, chopped
- 1 small handful of coriander (cilantro) leaves, chopped
- 1 tablespoon curry powder
- 1 teaspoon ground cumin
- 4 tablespoons olive oil

SERVES 4

Method

Heat a tablespoon of olive oil in a frying pan and add the mushrooms and spring onions (scallions). Cook for 2 minutes. Place the chickpeas (garbanzo beans) in a food processor along with the garlic and blitz until smooth. Transfer the mixture to a bowl and combine it with the onions, mushrooms, breadcrumbs, egg, herbs and spices. Shape the falafel mixture into patties. Heat 3 tablespoons of olive oil in the frying pan. Place the falafels into the pan and cook for around 5 minutes or until golden. Serve with salads or use in place of a beef burger.

Baked Ricotta & Green Salad

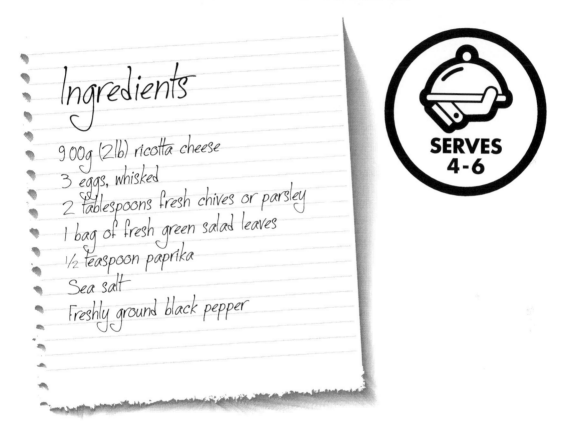

Ingredients

900g (2lb) ricotta cheese
3 eggs, whisked
2 tablespoons fresh chives or parsley
1 bag of fresh green salad leaves
1/2 teaspoon paprika
Sea salt
Freshly ground black pepper

SERVES 4-6

Method

Grease a loaf tin with a little oil. Place the ricotta cheese into a bowl and beat to make it soften. Pour in the eggs and combine with the cheese then add in the herbs and paprika and mix well. Season with salt and pepper. Scoop the mixture into the loaf tin and cook in the oven at 180C/360F for 30-35 minutes or until firm. Allow the baked ricotta to cool before removing it from the tin. Slice it and serve it with the salad leaves.

DINNER

Low Carb Lasagne

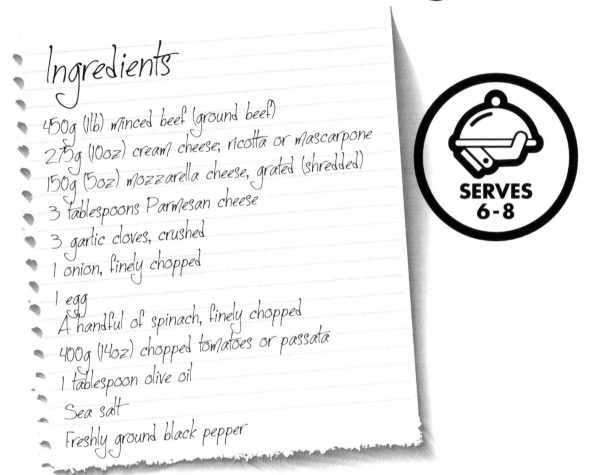

Ingredients

450g (1lb) minced beef (ground beef)

275g (10oz) cream cheese; ricotta or mascarpone

150g (5oz) mozzarella cheese, grated (shredded)

3 tablespoons Parmesan cheese

3 garlic cloves, crushed

1 onion, finely chopped

1 egg

A handful of spinach, finely chopped

400g (14oz) chopped tomatoes or passata

1 tablespoon olive oil

Sea salt

Freshly ground black pepper

SERVES 6-8

Method

Heat the olive oil in a large saucepan, add the beef and cook it for 5 minutes. Add in the garlic, tomatoes/ passata and season with salt and pepper. In the meantime place the cream cheese in a bowl and beat it to soften it. Add the egg and combine it with the cream cheese. Stir the spinach into the cheese mixture. Spoon HALF the meat mixture into a casserole dish and spread the cheese/ spinach mixture on top. Add another layer of meat and sprinkle over half the mozzarella, followed by another layer of meat. Finish it off with mozzarella and a sprinkling of parmesan. Transfer the lasagne to a pre-heated oven and cook at 180C/360F for 30 minutes until golden. Serve with a heap of green salad leaves.

Fresh Baked Scallops

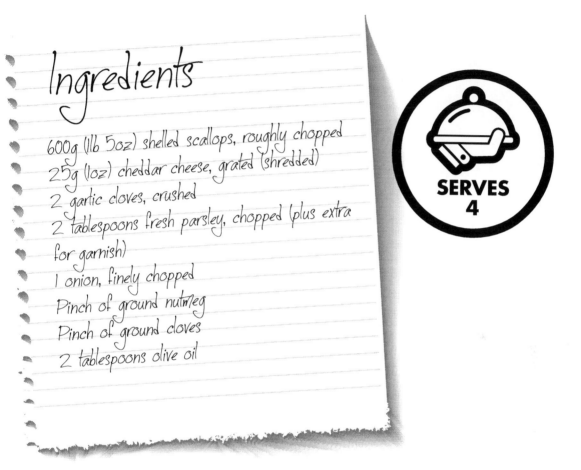

Ingredients

600g (1lb 5oz) shelled scallops, roughly chopped
25g (1oz) cheddar cheese, grated (shredded)
2 garlic cloves, crushed
2 tablespoons fresh parsley, chopped (plus extra
for garnish)
1 onion, finely chopped
Pinch of ground nutmeg
Pinch of ground cloves
2 tablespoons olive oil

SERVES 4

Method

Place the chopped scallops, garlic, onion, parsley, cloves and nutmeg into a bowl and
mix well. Spoon the mixture into 4 clean scallop shells or ovenproof serving dishes. Pour
½ tablespoon of olive oil on top of each shell/dish. Sprinkle with cheese and parsley.
Transfer them to the oven and bake at 200C/400F for around 20 minutes or until golden.

Prawn & Pea Pasta

Ingredients

350g (12oz) fusilli whole-wheat pasta
350g (12oz) prawns, peeled and cooked
200g (7oz) peas
1 small onion, chopped
2 tablespoons fresh parsley, chopped
1 tablespoon olive oil
Small pinch of saffron
200mls (7fl oz) stock (broth)

SERVES 4

Method

Heat the oil in a saucepan, add the onion and cook for 5 minutes until soft. Stir in the peas and prawns and cook for 3 minutes. Cook the pasta according to the instructions. In the meantime, pour the stock (broth) and saffron into the frying pan. Cook until the liquid has reduced to approximately half. Add in the cooked pasta and sprinkle with parsley. Season if required. Serve and enjoy.

Bacon Crusted Meatloaf

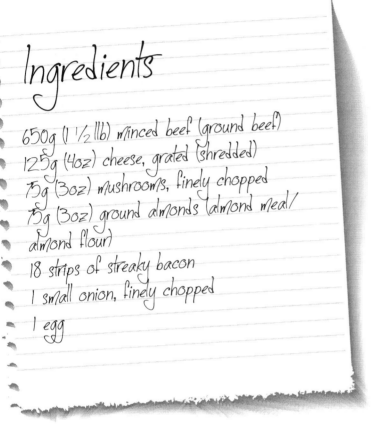

Ingredients

650g (1 1/2 llb) minced beef (ground beef)
125g (4oz) cheese, grated (shredded)
75g (3oz) mushrooms, finely chopped
75g (3oz) ground almonds (almond meal/
almond flour)
18 strips of streaky bacon
1 small onion, finely chopped
1 egg

**SERVES
4-6**

Method

Place the meat, mushrooms, onion, almonds, cheese and egg in a food processor and combine them. Line a loaf tin with cling film, press the mixture into the tin and cover it with film too. This is to get the shape of the loaf first. Remove the meat loaf from the tin and place it on a wire rack on a baking tray. Remove the plastic film. Lay the bacon rashers over the meat loaf, completely covering it and tucking the edges of the bacon underneath the loaf. Bake the meat loaf in an oven pre-heated to 180C/360F for 1 hour, or until the meat is completely cooked.

Aubergine & Mozzarella Stacks

Ingredients

150g (5oz) mozzarella cheese, grated (shredded)
8 tomatoes, finely chopped
4 tablespoons pine nuts
2 aubergines (eggplants), cut into 2cm (1 inch) slices
2 tablespoons olive oil
1 handful of basil leaves, chopped

FOR THE TOMATO SAUCE
1 x 400g (14oz) tin of tomatoes
1 teaspoon mixed herbs
2 tablespoons olive oil

SERVES 4

Method

Heat 2 tablespoons of oil in a pan, add the aubergine (eggplant) and cook for 3 minutes on each side.
Remove and set aside. In a bowl, combine the tomatoes, mozzarella and basil. Dry fry the pine nuts
for 1 minute until lightly toasted and mix them with the tomatoes and mozzarella. On a baking sheet,
place the 4 largest slices of aubergine and add a spoonful of the tomato, cheese and basil mixture.
Select the next largest pieces, place them on top, followed by more tomato mixture. Continue stacking
until you have 4 slices of aubergine piled up with the tomato mixture in between. Bake in the oven at
180/360F for 12 minutes. In the meantime, process the tomatoes, mixed herbs and olive oil in a blender
until smooth. Transfer to a saucepan and heat the sauce. Serve the stacked aubergine drizzled with the
tomato sauce.

Pork With Orange & Ginger

Ingredients

450g (1lb) pork fillet, cut into strips
4 spring onions (scallions) finely chopped
1 carrot, peeled and cut into strips
2.5cm (1 inch) chunk of ginger root, peeled
and finely chopped
1 teaspoon cornflour
1 tablespoon soy sauce
2 teaspoons ground nut oil
Zest and juice of 1 orange

SERVES 4

Method

Place the orange zest and juice, ginger and soy sauce into a bowl and add the pork strips. Allow them to marinate for 30 minutes or longer if you can. Stir in the cornflour. Heat the ground nut oil in a frying pan, add in the pork and cook for 1 minute. Stir in the carrots and spring onion (scallion) and cook until the vegetables have softened. Serve with brown rice or noodles.

Chickpea & Vegetable Casserole

SERVES 4

Ingredients

400g (14oz) tinned chickpeas (garbanzo beans) rinsed and drained

400g (14oz) chopped tinned tomatoes

3 large carrots, chopped

3 cloves of garlic, chopped

2 stalks celery, finely chopped

2 tablespoons freshly chopped parsley

1 bouquet garni

1 onion, finely chopped

1 courgette (zucchini), chopped

900mls (1 ½ pints) vegetable stock

4 tablespoons olive oil

Method

Heat the oil in a saucepan and add the onion and garlic. Cook gently for 5 minutes. Add in the carrots, celery and tomatoes. Cook for another 5 minutes. Add the chickpeas (garbanzo beans), courgette, bouquet garni and stock (broth) to the saucepan. Simmer for 15 minutes. Remove the bouquet garni. Sprinkle in the parsley and serve with baked potatoes.

Roast Autumn Vegetables

Ingredients

250g (9 oz) peas, fresh or frozen
150g (5oz) button mushrooms
3 tablespoons toasted seed mix; sesame seeds,
pumpkin seeds or flaxseeds
2 whole beetroot, unpeeled
2 cloves of garlic
1 butternut squash, peeled and cut into chunks
1 head of broccoli
2 tablespoons olive oil or ground nut oil
Sea salt
Freshly ground black pepper

**SERVES
4**

Method

Wash the beetroot then place it on a baking tray and sprinkle with salt. Place it in the oven at 200C/400F for around 1 hour or until tender. Place the squash on a separate baking tray and coat it with a little olive oil then transfer it to the oven and bake for around 45 minutes or until tender. In the meantime, steam the broccoli and peas for 5 minutes. Once the roast vegetables are cooked, heat the olive oil in a frying pan and add the garlic and mushrooms. Cook for around 3 minutes. Chop the beetroot and squash chunks and combine with the other vegetables. Sprinkle over the mixed seeds. Season with black pepper and serve.

Lamb Shanks & Lentils

Ingredients

4 lamb shanks
450g (1lb) puy lentils
4 carrots, chopped
4 cloves of garlic, crushed
1 onion, finely chopped
4 tablespoons tomato purée (paste)
3 bay leaves
1 bouquet garni
1800mls (3 pints) beef or vegetable stock (broth)
4 tablespoons olive oil

SERVES 4

Method

Heat the oil in a large saucepan, add the lamb, turning occasionally until it is brown all over. Remove it and set aside. Add the onion, carrots and garlic to the saucepan and cook for 5 minutes. Return the lamb to the saucepan and add in the stock (broth), tomato purée (paste), bouquet garni, bay leaves and lentils. Transfer it to an oven-proof dish, cover and cook in the oven at 200C/400F for 2 hours. Check half way through cooking and add extra stock (broth) or water if necessary. Serve and enjoy.

Chilli Bean Bake

Ingredients

400g (14oz) chopped tomatoes
400g (14oz) haricot beans
125g (5oz) rolled oats
50g (2oz) Cheddar cheese, grated (shredded)
100g (3 ½ oz) peas
3 handfuls of spinach leaves
2 cloves garlic, crushed
1 onion, chopped
4 tablespoons olive oil
1 tablespoon soy sauce
1 teaspoon chilli flakes
1 teaspoon dried oregano

SERVES 4

Method

Heat the olive oil in a frying pan, add the garlic, onion, chilli and oregano. Cook for 5 minutes. Add in the chopped tomatoes, oats and beans and cook for 5 minutes. Stir in the peas, spinach and soy sauce. Transfer the mixture to an ovenproof dish and sprinkle with cheese. Bake in the oven at 200C/400F for 10 minutes until the cheese is bubbling.

Fish Pie

Ingredients

700g (1lb 9 oz) filleted white fish, cod or haddock

200g (7oz) prawns, peeled and cooked

700g (1lb 9 oz) cooked potatoes, mashed

25g (1oz) cornflour

4 tablespoons fresh parsley, chopped

2 bay leaves

1 small onion, roughly chopped

1 sprig of thyme

1 teaspoon lemon zest

600mls (1 pint) milk

SERVES 6

Method

Place the milk in a saucepan with the onion, bay leaves, thyme and lemon zest. Add the fish and bring to the boil. Gently simmer for 15 minutes until the fish is cooked through. Strain the milk off the fish and set aside, ready to make the sauce. Discard the onion, bay leaves, thyme and zest. Flake the fish into chunks and place in an oven-proof casserole dish. To make the sauce, mix the cornflour with a splash of milk to make a paste. Stir the paste into the milk you set aside. Place it on the heat and stir until it thickens. Add in the parsley and prawns. Stir and cook for 2 minutes. Pour the sauce over the fish. Top it off with mashed potatoes. Transfer the fish pie to the oven and cook for 30 minutes at 180C/360F until the mashed potato is slightly golden.

Turkey & Spring Vegetable Casserole

Ingredients

- 675g (1 ½ lb) new potatoes
- 225g (8oz) carrots, chopped
- 225g (8oz) asparagus, chopped
- 200g (7oz) sugar-snap peas
- 4 turkey steaks
- 1 large onion, chopped
- 1 bay leaf
- 1 handful of tarragon, chopped
- 300mls (½ pint) chicken stock (broth)
- 175mls (6fl oz) crème fraiche
- 4 tablespoons olive oil

SERVES 4

Method

Heat the olive oil in a pan, add the turkey and onion and cook for around 5 minutes. Stir in the carrots, potatoes and cook for 3 minutes. Pour in the stock (broth) and add the bay leaf. Cook for 20 minutes or until the potatoes are soft. Add the asparagus and sugar-snap peas and cook for 4 minutes. Stir in the crème fraiche and tarragon. Remove the bay leaf and serve.

Chinese Style Quinoa Salad

Ingredients

- 300g (11oz) quinoa
- 150g (5oz) peas
- 5 radishes, chopped
- 1 large carrot, grated (shredded)
- 1 red pepper (bell pepper) chopped
- ½ cucumber, diced
- Handful of cashew nuts

FOR THE DRESSING:

- 1cm (½ inch) chunk of fresh ginger, grated (shredded)
- ½ -1 teaspoon chilli flakes (or according to taste)
- 3 tablespoons soy sauce
- 1 tablespoon olive oil
- 1 tablespoon sesame oil

SERVES 4

Method

Boil the quinoa for around 12 minutes or until the grains have opened and then drain it. Combine all of the vegetables and nuts in a large bowl and stir in the quinoa. In separate bowl mix together the ingredients for the dressing. Pour the dressing onto the salad and mix well.

Shepherd's Pie

Ingredients

800g (1¾lb) potatoes, peeled and chopped into small cubes

125g (4oz) streaky bacon, chopped

450g (1lb) minced beef (ground beef)

50g (2oz) cheese, grated (shredded)

1 garlic clove, chopped finely

1 onion, chopped finely

1 tablespoon fresh parsley, chopped

2 tablespoons tomato purée (paste)

2 tablespoons butter

½ teaspoon sea salt

½ teaspoon white pepper

Pinch of nutmeg

SERVES 4-6

Method

In a large pan, fry the bacon until crispy and set aside. Add the beef to the frying pan and cook for 2 minutes. Add the garlic, onion, tomato puree (paste), parsley, salt and pepper. Cover and cook on a low heat for 30 minutes, stirring occasionally. Meanwhile, boil the potatoes for around 10 minutes or until tender. Drain them, add the butter, nutmeg and mash them. Preheat the oven to 230C/450F. Spread the beef mixture onto the bottom of an ovenproof casserole dish. Add the mashed potato layer on top and smooth out with the back of a spoon. Sprinkle with cheese and bake in the oven for around 20 minutes or until the pie is lightly browned and the cheese melted.

Chorizo & Roast Vegetables

Ingredients

1 large chorizo sausage, roughly chopped

4 cloves garlic, chopped

2 aubergines (eggplants), sliced

1 butternut squash, peeled de-seeded and chopped

1 red pepper (bell pepper), sliced

1 green pepper (bell pepper), sliced

1 yellow pepper (bell pepper) sliced

1 onion, chopped

1 teaspoon ground coriander (cilantro)

1 handful of fresh basil or marjoram, chopped

2 tablespoons balsamic vinegar

2 tablespoons olive oil

SERVES 4

Method

Place all of the vegetables into a roasting tin and sprinkle in the coriander (cilantro), olive oil and balsamic vinegar. Apart from the fresh herbs, toss everything together and make sure it's well coated. Add in the chorizo sausage. Roast in the oven at 220C/425F for 25-30 minutes or until the vegetables have softened and are caramelised. Stir in the fresh herbs. Serve with a green leafy salad. As an alternative the vegetables can be topped with grated cheese.

Pork Koftas & Roast Pepper Salad

Ingredients

450g (1lb) pork mince (ground pork)
3 red peppers (bell peppers), halved and deseeded
2 large handfuls of lettuce leaves
2 teaspoons ground cumin
2 teaspoons ground coriander (cilantro)
1 onion, finely chopped
1 egg white
1 teaspoon cayenne pepper
1 handful of fresh parsley, chopped
1 tablespoon olive oil
FOR THE DRESSING:
200g (7oz) Greek yogurt
1 clove of garlic, crushed
2 tablespoons fresh parsley, chopped
1 tablespoon lemon juice

**SERVES
4**

Method

Place the peppers (bell peppers) under a hot grill (broiler) and cook until the skin is charred. Place them in a bag for 3 minutes until the skin loosens then peel it off. Chop them and set aside. Heat the oil in a pan, add the onion and cook until softened. Stir in the spices and cook for 2 minutes. In a bowl, combine the onion, pork, egg white and parsley. Make the mixture into 8 sausage shapes and slide them onto skewers. Place them under a hot grill for about 8 minutes, turning until completely cooked. Combine the dressing ingredients into a bowl. Serve the lettuce leaves and chopped peppers onto plates. Add the koftas and serve with the dressing.

Smokey Bean & Mushroom Stew

Ingredients

400g (14oz) black-eyed peas
400g (14oz) haricot beans
400g (14oz) tinned tomatoes, chopped
225g (8oz) chestnut mushrooms, sliced
2 garlic cloves, chopped
2 onions, chopped
1 tablespoon smoked paprika
1 red chilli, finely chopped
1 large handful of parsley
250mls (8fl oz) vegetable stock (broth)
1 tablespoon soy sauce
1 tablespoon olive oil

SERVES 4

Method

Heat the oil in a saucepan, add the onions and garlic and cook for 4 minutes until the onions have softened. Stir in the mushrooms, chilli, haricot beans, black-eyed peas, tomatoes, paprika and soy sauce and cook for 5 minutes. Pour in the stock (broth) and simmer for 15 minutes. Stir in the parsley and serve into bowls

Chicken & Vegetable Bake

SERVES 4

Ingredients

225g (8oz) new potatoes, chopped

20 cherry tomatoes

20 pitted black olives

8 chicken thighs

2 stalks of celery, roughly chopped

1 red pepper (bell pepper), de-seeded and chopped

1 aubergine (eggplant), cut into chunks

1 onion, roughly chopped

1 teaspoon mixed herbs

1 teaspoon paprika

3 tablespoons olive oil

Juice of ½ lemon

Handful of fresh basil leaves

Method

Place the olive oil, paprika and lemon juice into a bowl and stir. Place the potatoes and vegetables, except for the olives and tomatoes, into a large oven-proof dish and pour around half of the paprika oil mixture over them. Add the chicken thighs on top of the vegetables and drizzle the remaining paprika oil over the chicken. Sprinkle in the dried herbs. Cover the dish with foil and bake in the oven at 200C/400F for 30 minutes. Remove the foil from the dish, add the tomatoes and olives and cook for another 15 minutes. Check the chicken is cooked through and the vegetables are soft. Sprinkle with basil leaves and serve.

Fillet Steak With Garlic & Chive Butter

SERVES 4

Ingredients

4 fillet steaks
2 tablespoons olive oil
Sea salt
Freshly ground black pepper

FOR THE GARLIC & CHIVE BUTTER.
125g (4oz) soft butter
3 cloves of garlic, crushed
1 tablespoon fresh chives, chopped

Method

Place the butter in a bowl with the garlic and chives and combine until smooth. Chill the butter in the fridge for 20 minutes. Sprinkle the steaks with salt and pepper. Heat the olive oil in a frying pan and add the steaks. Cook them to your liking. As a guide 2½ minutes each side for rare, 3½ minutes each side for medium rare and 4½ minutes each side for medium. Serve the steaks with a large spoonful of garlic butter on top. Allow them to rest for 5 minutes before eating.

Feta Celeriac Bake

Ingredients

100g (3 ½ oz) feta cheese, crumbled
2 tablespoons butter
2 cloves of garlic, peeled
1 celeriac, peeled and chopped
1 tablespoon crème fraiche
Knob of butter for greasing
Sea salt
Freshly ground black pepper

SERVES
6

Method

Place the garlic and celeriac into a saucepan, cover with water, bring to the boil and cook for around 12 minutes or until the celeriac is tender. Drain the water off the celeriac. Add 2 tablespoons of butter and the crème fraiche and mash until the celeriac is soft and smooth. Stir in the crumbled feta until it's evenly dispersed in the mash. Grease a baking dish with a knob of butter then transfer the celeriac mash into the dish. Place little pieces of butter on top of the bake. Season with salt and pepper. Transfer to the oven and bake for 30 minutes at 200C/400F. Serve alongside meat dishes.

Creole Chicken

Ingredients

4 chicken breasts
250g (9 oz) mange tout (snow peas)
2 x 400g (14oz) tinned chopped tomatoes
4 cloves garlic, chopped
1 tablespoon curry powder
1 teaspoon ground cumin
½ teaspoon paprika
200mls (7fl oz) chicken stock (broth)
3 tablespoons olive oil

SERVES 4

Method

Heat the oil in a frying pan, add the chicken, cumin, paprika and curry powder and cook until the chicken is browned. Add the garlic, tomatoes and stock (broth). Bring to the boil then reduce the heat and simmer for 25 minutes. Stir in the mange tout (snow peas) and cook for 10 minutes. Serve with brown rice.

King Prawns & Garlic Dip

Ingredients

425g (15oz) king prawns, peeled
150g (5oz) cream cheese
150g (5oz) Greek yogurt
2 cloves of garlic, crushed
2 teaspoons fresh dill, finely chopped
1 red chilli, finely chopped
1 tablespoon coconut oil
Squeeze of lemon juice
Sea salt

SERVES 4

Method

In a bowl, combine the yogurt, cream cheese, garlic and lemon juice. Season with sea salt. Spoon the dip into a serving bowl. Heat the coconut oil in a frying pan, add the prawns and cook for around 7-8 minutes until they are cooked through and pink. Arrange the prawns on a plate and sprinkle with dill and chopped chilli ready to be shared.

Lemon Risotto

Ingredients

1 tablespoon butter
1 onion, finely chopped
Zest and juice of 1 lemon
3 tablespoons olive oil
2 cloves of garlic, crushed
225g (8oz) risotto rice (Arborio)
750ml (1¼ pint) warm chicken stock (broth)
40g (1½oz) Parmesan cheese, grated
3 tablespoons pine nuts
1 tablespoon fresh parsley, chopped
Sea salt & freshly ground black pepper

SERVES 4

Method

Heat the butter and oil in a pan. Add the onion and garlic and cook until the onion is soft. Add the rice and stir. Add the lemon juice and zest. Mix it together. Add in the stock (broth) a little at a time until the rice absorbs all of it. It should take around 20 minutes. Once the rice is soft and creamy, add in the pine nuts, Parmesan and parsley. Season with salt and pepper and serve.

Fast Chicken Curry

Ingredients

4 chicken breasts, cubed
3 tablespoons mild curry powder
1 onion, chopped
1 teaspoon ground coriander (cilantro)
1 bay leaf
1 teaspoon ground ginger
600mls (1 pint) chicken stock (broth)
2 tablespoons olive oil

SERVES 4

Method

Heat the oil in a frying pan, add the onion and cook until it softens. Add the coriander (cilantro), curry powder, ginger and the bay leaf and cook for 5 minutes. Add the chicken and chicken stock (broth). Cook for 15 minutes or until the chicken is cooked thoroughly. Remove the bay leaf and serve with brown rice.

Roast Red Pepper Chicken

Ingredients

4 large chicken breasts
3 tablespoons fresh coriander (cilantro)
2 cloves of garlic, crushed
2 tomatoes, chopped
1 red pepper (bell pepper)
1 yellow pepper (bell pepper)
1 onion, chopped
300mls (½ pint) chicken stock (broth)
4 tablespoon olive oil
Sea salt
Freshly ground black pepper

SERVES 4

Method

Heat the olive oil in a frying pan, add the chicken and brown it for 5 minutes. Add the garlic and onions and cook for 5 minutes. Add the peppers (bell peppers), tomatoes and chicken stock (broth) bring it to the boil, reduce the heat and simmer for 15 minutes. Stir in the fresh coriander (cilantro) and season with salt and pepper. Serve with avocado and salad.

Grilled Courgette Cheese

Ingredients

150g (5oz) Cheddar cheese, grated (shredded)
2 courgettes (zucchinis), sliced into 2 cm
(1 inch) pieces
2 tablespoons butter
1 teaspoon chives (optional)

SERVES 2-4

Method

Heat the butter in a large frying pan. Add the courgette (zucchini) and cook for around 4 minutes until it softens. Transfer the courgette slices to a baking sheet and sprinkle over the cheese and chives (if using). Place under a hot grill (broiler) for 3-4 minutes until the cheese melts. Serve as an accompaniment to meat, fish and salads instead of potatoes, rice or pasta.

Roast Garlic & Rosemary Lamb

SERVES 4-6

Ingredients

3 cloves of garlic, chopped
1 leg of lamb
1-2 tablespoons fresh rosemary leaves, finely chopped
2 tablespoons butter
Sea salt
Freshly ground black pepper

Method

Place the garlic and rosemary in a pestle in mortar and grind to a smooth paste. Mix it with the butter until well combined. Make several incisions in the lamb and press the herby butter into the cuts and spread the rest over the lamb. Season the lamb with salt and pepper. Place the lamb in a roasting tin and cook until the lamb is done to your liking. It will take around 20 minutes for each 450g (1lb) of meat. Serve with vegetables or salad.

Sweet Potato & Spring Onion Mash

Ingredients

700g (1lb 9 oz) sweet potato, peeled and chopped

1 bunch of spring onions (scallion), finely chopped

½ teaspoon ground nutmeg

2 teaspoons butter

Sea salt

Freshly ground black pepper

SERVES 4-6

Method

Place the sweet potatoes in a saucepan, bring to the boil and simmer for 10-12 minutes, until soft. Drain the sweet potatoes but leave them in the saucepan. Add the spring onions (scallions), nutmeg and butter. Mash until the sweet potatoes are smooth. Season and serve.

Pork In Mushroom Cream Sauce

Ingredients

6 large mushrooms, sliced
4 boneless pork chops
2 medium shallots, finely chopped
180mls (6fl oz) double cream (heavy cream)
2 tablespoons olive oil
Sea salt
Freshly ground black pepper

SERVES 4

Method

Heat the oil in a large frying pan over a medium-high heat. Add the chops reduce the heat and fry for 3 or 4 minutes per side, or until cooked through. Transfer the chops to a plate and cover with foil to keep them warm. Reduce the heat of the frying pan and add the mushrooms and shallots to the pan. Cook until softened. Pour in the cream and season with salt and pepper. Stir until warmed through. Serve the pork chops with the pepper sauce.

Beef Stew In A Pumpkin

Ingredients

900g (2lbs) beef, cut into chunks
3 tablespoons vegetable oil
200mls (7fl oz) water
3 large potatoes, peeled and cut into chunks
4 carrots, peeled and chopped
3 cloves of garlic, crushed
1 onion, chopped
1 beef stock (broth) cube
1 large pumpkin approx (10lb), washed, top cut off and set aside, seeds and stringy pieces removed
1 teaspoon sea salt
1/2 teaspoon pepper
400g (14oz) tin of chopped tomatoes

SERVES 8-10

Method

Heat 2 tablespoons of vegetable oil in a saucepan, add the meat and brown it for 5 minutes. Add in the potatoes, carrots, garlic, onion, water, salt and pepper. Cook for 25 minutes. Stir in the stock cubes and tomatoes. Place the pumpkin on a baking tray and brush it with a tablespoon of vegetable oil. Transfer the stew into the pumpkin and place the lid on top. Bake in the oven at 170C/325F for around 2 hours or until the pumpkin is tender, being careful not to overcook it. Serve directly from the pumpkin. Although this dish may take a while to cook, it's well worth it and will likely become a family favourite!

Chicken & Bean Bake

Ingredients

1 aubergine (eggplant), sliced
450g (1lb) chicken breast, cubed
1 onion, chopped
400g (14oz) tinned tomatoes
400g (14oz) kidney beans
250g (9 oz) Cheddar cheese, grated (shredded)
1 teaspoon paprika
1 teaspoon chilli powder
1/2 teaspoon garlic powder
1/4 teaspoon ground nutmeg
1 tablespoon olive oil
Sea salt
Freshly ground black pepper

SERVES 4-6

Method

Heat the olive oil in a frying pan, add the chicken and brown it then add in the onion and cook for 3 minutes. Add to the pan the tomatoes, kidney beans, garlic powder, chilli and paprika. Bring to the boil and season with salt and pepper. Place the chicken in a casserole dish and add a layer of aubergines then a layer of chicken and a layer of aubergine. Sprinkle the cheese over the top and season with nutmeg. Transfer the casserole to the oven and bake at 190C/375F for 50 minutes or until the top is slightly golden.

Thai Pork Parcels

Ingredients

450g (1lb) minced pork
3 garlic cloves, crushed
2 inner stalks lemongrass, finely chopped
1 onion, finely chopped
1 bunch mint, finely chopped
1 bunch coriander (cilantro), finely chopped
1 cucumber, peeled
1 spring onion (scallion), finely sliced
1 tablespoon fish sauce
Few heads baby gem lettuce
Juice of 1 lemon

SERVES 4

Method

Place the pork, garlic, lemongrass, onion and fish sauce into a bowl and combine them well. Shape the mixture into patties and place them on a lightly greased baking tray. Transfer them to the oven and bake at 200C/400F for 15–20 minutes. Meanwhile, you can make little salad boats to serve them in. Grate (shred) a cucumber without the skin and mix with the sliced spring onion (scallion). Serve the pork parcels into the lettuce leaves and add the cucumber and spring onion. Sprinkle with coriander (cilantro) and mint and a squeeze of lemon juice.

Parmesan Pumpkin

Ingredients

1.6kg (3½ lb) pumpkin, peeled, de-seeded and sliced
50g (2oz) breadcrumbs
50g (2oz) parmesan cheese, grated (shredded)
2 eggs, whisked
2 tablespoons fresh basil leaves
1 onion, finely chopped
1 clove garlic, chopped
400mls (14fl oz) passata
4 tablespoons olive oil

SERVES 6

Method

Heat the oil in a saucepan, add the garlic and onion and cook for 5 minutes. Stir in the passata and basil. Simmer for 10 minutes.

Whisk the eggs in a bowl and place the breadcrumbs onto a plate. Dunk the slices of pumpkin into the egg and then dip them in the breadcrumbs. Heat the oil in a frying pan and cook the pumpkin until golden. Transfer them to an ovenproof dish, cover with passata and sprinkle with Parmesan. Bake in the oven at 180C/360F for around 20 minutes.

Slow Cooked Spiced Lamb

SERVES 4-6

Ingredients

1.35kg (3lb) lamb shoulder
2 tablespoons olive oil
½ teaspoon ground cumin
½ teaspoon ground coriander (cilantro)
½ teaspoon ground cinnamon
½ teaspoon paprika
3 tablespoons butter

Method

In a bowl combine the spices with the butter. Coat the lamb with the spiced butter mixture and marinate it for an hour, or longer if you can. Heat the oil in a pan, add the lamb and brown it for 3-4 minutes on all sides to seal it. Place the lamb in an ovenproof dish and cover it with foil. Transfer the lamb to the oven and roast at 170C/325F for 4 hours. The lamb should be tender and falling off the bone. Shred the lamb and serve onto a dish. Alternatively the lamb can be cooked in a slow cooker.

Coconut Crumb Prawns

Ingredients

450g (1lb) large prawns (shrimp), peeled but tails attached

100g (3½ oz) ground almonds (almond flour/ almond meal)

100g (3½ oz) desiccated (shredded) coconut

2 eggs, whisked

1-2 tablespoons coconut oil

½ teaspoon sea salt

½ teaspoon pepper

SERVES 4

Method

Place the ground almonds (almond flour/almond meal), salt and pepper into a bowl, in another bowl place the beaten egg and in another place the desiccated (shredded) coconut Dip the prawns (shrimp) in the ground almonds (almond flour/ almond meal) then dip them in the eggs and finally dredge it in the coconut making sure you get plenty of coconut onto each one for crispiness. Continue for each of the prawns and set them onto a plate. Heat the oil in a pan. Add a few prawns at a time and cook for around 2-3 minutes on each side. Serve with mayonnaise.

Spare Ribs

Ingredients

1kg (2lb 4oz) pork ribs, individually cut
2 teaspoons paprika
1 teaspoon ground ginger
1 teaspoon cinnamon
1/2 teaspoon ground star anise
1/4 teaspoon salt
1/2 teaspoon ground pepper
3 tablespoons ground nut oil

SERVES 4

Method

Place the spices, salt, pepper and oil into a bowl and combine. Coat the ribs with the mixture making sure they're evenly coated. Place the pork ribs in a roasting tin and cook them in the oven at 180C/360F for 35-40 minutes. Alternatively the ribs can be cooked on a barbecue once they've been coated. Place on a large serving plate and eat them while hot.

Sweet Potato & Spinach Bites

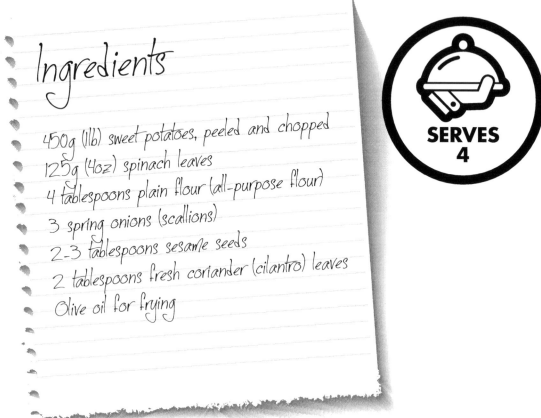

Ingredients

450g (1lb) sweet potatoes, peeled and chopped

125g (4oz) spinach leaves

4 tablespoons plain flour (all-purpose flour)

3 spring onions (scallions)

2-3 tablespoons sesame seeds

2 tablespoons fresh coriander (cilantro) leaves

Olive oil for frying

SERVES 4

Method

Boil the sweet potatoes for around 20 minutes until it's tender then drain them. Mash the potatoes and set aside. Dip the spinach in boiling water for around a minute until it has wilted. Drain the excess moisture off the spinach then combine it with the mashed sweet potato. Add the spring onion (scallions), coriander (cilantro) and combine. Form the mixture into small patties. Roll the patties in sesame seeds and flour. Heat the oil in a large frying pan. Carefully add the patties to the oil and cook them for around 3-4 minutes until they are crisp and golden. Serve with salsa or dips.

Chicken, Green Pepper & Olive Casserole

Ingredients

250g (9oz) button mushrooms
175g (6oz) green olives
4 large chicken breasts
2 cloves of garlic, crushed
2 green peppers (bell peppers), seeds removed & chopped
1 large onion, chopped
150mls (5fl oz) chicken stock (broth)
6 tablespoons double cream (heavy cream)
2 tablespoons olive oil
Sea salt, freshly ground black pepper
Chopped parsley to garnish

SERVES 4

Method

Heat the olive oil in a frying pan, add the chicken and brown it on both sides. Remove and set aside. Add the garlic and onion to the pan and cook for 2 minutes. Add the mushrooms and green pepper (bell peppers) to the pan and continue cooking for 2 minutes. Transfer the chicken and vegetables to an ovenproof casserole dish. Pour in the chicken stock (broth). Cover the casserole and bake in the oven at 180C/360F for around 45 minutes. Stir in the cream and the olives. Season with salt and pepper. Continue cooking for another 15 minutes. Garnish with parsley and serve.

Baked Chicory

Ingredients

4 chicory heads, quartered
2 tablespoons butter
100mls (3½ oz) double cream (heavy cream)
1 tablespoon olive oil
Sea salt
Freshly ground black pepper

SERVES 4

Method

Grease a casserole dish with the olive oil and place the chicory in the dish. Flake the butter over the chicory and season with a little salt and pepper. Cover the dish with foil and transfer it to the oven. Bake at 190C/375F for 45 minutes, basting the chicory occasionally. Remove it from the oven and add the cream to the chicory. Place it under a hot grill (broiler) until golden.

Five-Spice Pork Salad

Ingredients

4 boneless pork steaks, cut into strips
175g (6oz) lettuce, chopped
100g (3½ oz) mange tout (snow peas), sliced
2 stalks of celery, finely chopped
½ cucumber, finely chopped
3 teaspoons Chinese five-spice
3 tablespoons fish sauce
3 tablespoons rice vinegar
2 tablespoons sesame oil
2 tablespoons olive oil
2cm (1 inch) chunk fresh ginger, grated (shredded)
2 tablespoons fresh coriander (cilantro) chopped

SERVES 4

Method

Place the olive oil, fish sauce, five-spice, ginger and vinegar together in a bowl and mix well. Add the pork strips, coat them in the marinade then cover and chill for 1 hour, or longer if you can. Heat the sesame oil in a frying pan or wok. Add the pork and marinade and cook for 3-4 minutes or until cooked through. Combine the lettuce, celery, cucumber, mange tout (snow peas) and coriander (cilantro) in a bowl. Add in the cooked pork strips and the marinade juices. Serve with rice or noodles and eat immediately.

Pistachio Crusted Chicken

Ingredients

125g (4oz) pistachio nuts
12 chicken drumsticks, skin on
3 tablespoons ground almonds (almond flour/almond meal)
1 tablespoon medium curry powder
1 large handful of coriander (cilantro) leaves
1 large egg (or 2 small eggs), beaten
4 tablespoons olive oil

SERVES 4

Method

In a bowl, mix together the ground almonds (almond flour/almond meal) and curry powder. Coat the chicken drumsticks in the mixture and set aside. Place the pistachios, coriander (cilantro) and any leftover almond mixture into a blender and blitz it. Tip the mixture onto a plate. Dip the coated chicken drumsticks into beaten egg then coat them in the pistachio mixture. Place them on a baking sheet greased with the olive oil and transfer them to the oven. Roast the chicken in the oven at 220C/425F for around 30 minutes or until completely cooked. Serve with green salad.

Chicken Tikka

Ingredients

450g (1lb) chicken thighs, skin on
2.5cm (1 inch) chunk of fresh ginger root, finely
chopped
1 clove of garlic, crushed
1 teaspoon chilli powder
½ teaspoon sea salt
½ teaspoon turmeric
150mls (5fl oz) plain Greek yogurt
2 tablespoons olive oil
Juice of 1 lemon

SERVES 4

Method

Place the ginger, chilli, salt, turmeric, yogurt and lemon juice in a bowl and mix everything together. Stir in the chicken and allow to marinate for 1 hour or overnight if you have time. Baste the chicken in olive oil. Place the chicken under a hot grill (broiler) for around 15 minutes, turning occasionally and basting with oil during cooking.

DESSERTS, TREATS & SNACKS

Lemon Cheesecake

Ingredients

800g (1 3/4 lb) cream cheese, such as mascarpone

4 eggs

3 tablespoons lemon juice

2 teaspoons stevia (or to taste)

SERVES 8-10

Method

Place all of the ingredients into a bowl and combine them. Transfer the mixture to a pie dish and bake at 170C/325F for one hour. Remove the cheesecake and allow it to cool. Serve chilled.

Creamy Stuffed Peaches

Ingredients

4 large ripe peaches, halved and stone removed

100g (3½ oz) cream cheese

2 tablespoons oat bran

Zest of 1 orange

SERVES 4

Method

Place the peaches in an oven-proof dish with the flat side facing up. Place the orange zest, oat bran and cream cheese into a bowl and combine the ingredients. Spoon the creamy mixture into the centre of the peaches. Bake them in the oven at 180C/360F for 15 minutes. Serve them on their own or with a little crème fraiche or plain yogurt.

Chocolate Mousse

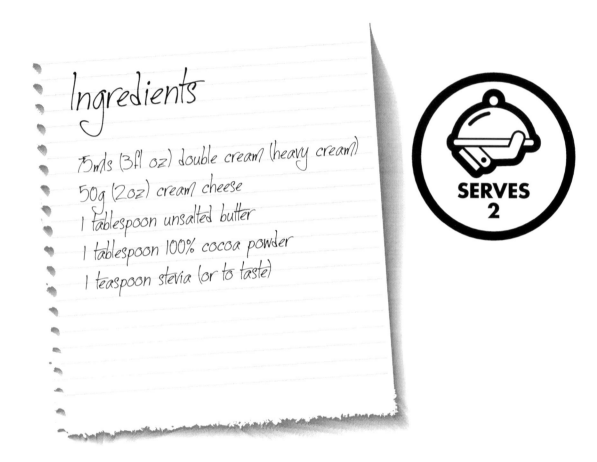

Ingredients

75mls (3fl oz) double cream (heavy cream)
50g (2oz) cream cheese
1 tablespoon unsalted butter
1 tablespoon 100% cocoa powder
1 teaspoon stevia (or to taste)

SERVES 2

Method

Place the butter and stevia into a bowl and mix until smooth. Stir in the cream cheese and cocoa powder and mix thoroughly. Whip the cream until thick and fold it into the mixture. Spoon the mousse into long stemmed glasses or serving bowls. Chill before serving.

Coconut Truffles

Ingredients

100g (3½ oz) mascarpone cheese
50g (2oz) creamed coconut
2 tablespoons desiccated (shredded) coconut
2 tablespoons coconut oil
Juice of ½ lemon
1 teaspoon stevia sweetener (or to taste)
Pinch of salt

FOR THE COATING:
50g (2oz) desiccated (shredded) coconut

Method

Place the mascarpone cheese, creamed coconut, 2 tablespoons of desiccated (shredded) coconut, stevia and coconut oil in a blender and blitz until smooth. Add in the salt and lemon juice and blend a little more. Chill the mixture for 40 minutes. Place the coconut for the coating into a plate. Scoop out a teaspoon of the mixture and shape it into a ball. Roll the ball in the 50g (2oz) coconut for the coating. Chill before serving.

Lemon & Blueberry Muffins

MAKES 12

Ingredients

125g (4oz) coconut flour
100g (3½ oz) blueberries
3 eggs, whisked
2 ripe bananas, mashed
4 tablespoons coconut oil
1 teaspoon vanilla extract
½ teaspoon baking powder
Pinch of salt
Zest and juice of a lemon

Method

Place the eggs and bananas into a bowl and beat them until creamy. Place the coconut flour in a separate bowl and add in the baking powder, coconut oil, lemon juice, vanilla extract and a pinch of salt and mix well. Add in the egg mixture and combine until smooth. Stir in the blueberries. Line a 12 muffin tin with paper cases and spoon in the mixture. Transfer the muffins to the oven and bake at 200C/400F for around 20 minutes.

Coffee Creams

Ingredients

250g (9 oz) ricotta cheese
150mls (5fl oz) double cream (heavy cream)
5 tablespoons black coffee
4 teaspoons stevia powder
1 tablespoon 100% cocoa powder plus extra to garnish

SERVES 4

Method

Mix together the coffee and stevia and stir it well. Place the ricotta into a bowl and beat it to soften it then pour in the coffee mixture and combine it. Whisk the double cream (heavy cream) until it forms soft peaks. Fold the whisked cream into the ricotta mixture and stir in the cocoa powder. Combine the mixture well. Spoon it into dessert glasses or decorative bowls. Sprinkle with a little cocoa powder and chill before serving.

Walnut & Banana Cake

Ingredients

250g (9 oz) plain flour (all-purpose flour)
2 bananas, peeled and mashed
125g (4oz) butter
125g (4oz) walnuts, chopped
3 eggs
175mls (6fl oz) water
2 teaspoons baking powder
1 teaspoon baking soda

SERVES 6

Method

Place the butter and bananas into a bowl and beat them until they are soft and creamy. Add in the eggs and mix well. Add in the flour, baking soda, baking powder to the banana mixture. Slowly add in the water and beat the mixture well then stir in the walnuts. Transfer the mixture into a greased baking tin. Place in an oven, preheated to 180C/360F and bake it for around 35 minutes. Test to see if it's cooked by using a skewer which should come out clean. Allow it to cool. Slice and serve.

Baked Raspberry Cheesecake

Ingredients

175g (6oz) mascarpone cheese
150g (5oz) full fat plain yogurt
1 tablespoon plain flour
(all-purpose flour)
1 teaspoon stevia (or to taste)
1 egg
1 egg white
200g (8oz) raspberries

SERVES
4-6

Method

Grease and line a cake tin of around 18cm in diameter. Place the mascarpone in a bowl and beat until smooth. Combine it with the yogurt, stevia, flour, egg, egg white and mix it until creamy. Stir in the raspberries then spoon the mixture into the cake tin. Place in an oven preheated to 180C/360F for around 30 minutes or until the cake has set completely. Serve warm with a few raspberries on the side and a little cream if required.

No-Bake Chocolate & Banana Flapjacks

SERVES 6-8

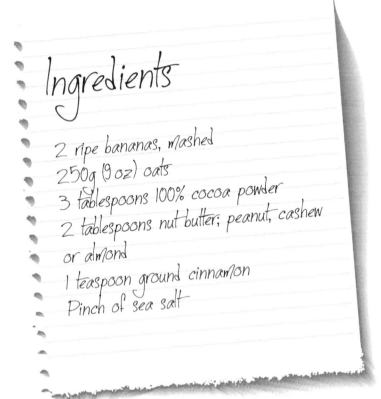

Ingredients

2 ripe bananas, mashed
250g (9 oz) oats
3 tablespoons 100% cocoa powder
2 tablespoons nut butter; peanut, cashew
or almond
1 teaspoon ground cinnamon
Pinch of sea salt

Method

Place all of the ingredients into a bowl and mix it really well. Scoop the mixture into a shallow tin and smooth it down well. Cover the mixture and chill before cutting into slices and serving. If you like you can experiment by adding additional ingredients, chopped nuts, coconut or protein powder.

Coconut Power Truffles

Ingredients

250g (9 oz) ground almonds (almond flour/almond meal)
75g (3oz) desiccated (shredded) coconut
3 tablespoons chia seeds
4 tablespoons 100% cocoa powder
1 banana, mashed
1 tablespoon coconut oil
1/2 teaspoon vanilla extract
Pinch of salt

Method

Place the chia seeds in a large bowl with 2 tablespoons of water and let it sit for around 15 minutes until it thickens. Place all of the ingredients into a bowl and combine them well until the mixture is well blended and thick. Using a teaspoon, scoop out the mixture and roll it in your (clean) hands to shape it into balls. Place the truffles on a baking sheet and cook them at 190C/375F for 15 minutes.

High Protein Chocolate Peanut Butter Biscuits

Ingredients

225g (8oz) tinned chickpeas (garbanzo beans), well drained
125g (4oz) peanut butter
3 tablespoons 100% cocoa powder
1 teaspoon vanilla extract
1 teaspoon stevia sweetener (optional)
200mls (7fl oz) almond milk
1 teaspoon baking powder

Method

Place all of the ingredients into a blender and process until smooth. You can add a little extra almond milk to thin the mixture if required. Scoop out spoonfuls of the mixture and place them on a baking tray. Transfer them to an oven, preheated to 200C/400F and cook for 15 minutes.

Apple Pie & Cinnamon Cream

Ingredients

FOR THE BASE:

250g (9 oz) pecan nuts, ground

1 tablespoon butter

1 teaspoon vanilla extract

1 teaspoon ground cinnamon

2 tablespoons water

Pinch of salt

FOR THE FILLING:

8 sweet apples, peeled, cored and finely sliced

1 1/2 teaspoons ground cinnamon

FOR THE CREAM:

400mls (14fl oz) double cream (whipping cream)

1/2 teaspoon cinnamon

Method

Place all the ingredients for the base into a blender and process until smooth. Transfer the mixture to a pie dish and press it down well. Place the dish in an oven pre-heated to 190C/375F and bake for 10 minutes. Remove the base and layer the apple slices over it, sprinkling cinnamon in the layers. Lower the temperature of the oven to 180C/360F, cover the pie with foil and bake it for 45-50 minutes until slightly golden. Remove the foil for the last 5 minutes of baking. Whisk the cream until thick and stir in the cinnamon. Serve the apple pie hot with a dollop of cinnamon cream.

Chive & Broad Bean Dip

Ingredients

225g (8oz) frozen peas
225g (8oz) broad beans
2 tablespoons fresh chives
1 avocado
1 tablespoon lemon juice
Freshly ground black pepper

Method

Boil the peas and beans in water until warmed through then drain them and allow them to cool. Place all of the ingredients into a blender and process until smooth. Transfer the dip to a bowl and chill before serving. It's delicious served as a dip for crudités

Parmesan Crisps

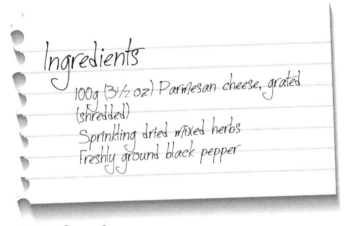

Ingredients

100g (3½ oz) Parmesan cheese, grated (shredded)
Sprinkling dried mixed herbs
Freshly ground black pepper

SERVES
2

Method

Place small separate circular amounts of cheese on a baking sheet and sprinkle with a pinch of herbs. Season with pepper. Transfer them to the oven and bake at 150C/300F for around 5 minutes until they become golden and crisp. Delicious on their own or served with dips.

20005383R00061

Printed in Great Britain
by Amazon